This edition published 1991
by the Promotional Reprint Company Limited
for Magna Books, Magna Road, Leicester, U.K.
ISBN 1-85422-226-0

opqrstuvwxyz

abcdefghijklmn

Purnell's
Illustrated
Children's
Dictionary

Compiled by Betty Root

Tutor-in-charge, Reading and Language Information Centre
Reading University School of Education

Illustrated by Hutchings

opqrstuvwxyz

All the words in the first part of this illustrated picture dictionary give the names of things. Words which are names are called nouns. Every single word is illustrated with a clear picture and this will help you to understand the meaning of the word.

Because this is a dictionary, the words are in the same order as the alphabet. If you want to know how to spell a word or to find out what it means it will be easy for you to look it up.

Remember words which are names of things and people are called nouns.

abcdefghijklmn

opqrstuvwxyz

A a

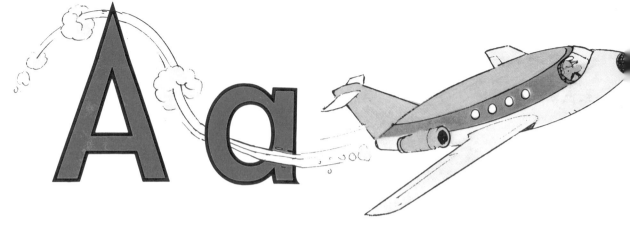

acorn The nut which grows on an oak tree. If you plant an acorn it will take a long time to grow into a tree.

aeroplane A machine which flies in the sky.

alligator An animal which lives in rivers and looks like a crocodile.

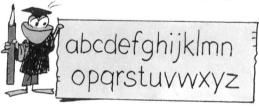

abcdefghijklmn opqrstuvwxyz

alphabet The letters which are used to write words. These letters go in a special order.

acrobat An acrobat does clever tricks at the circus.

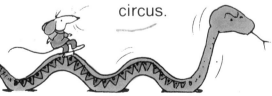

alsatian A large dog which looks a bit like a wolf.

adder A poisonous snake.

abcdefghijklmn

ambulance A special kind of car which takes people to hospital when they are ill or hurt.

anchor A heavy piece of iron on a long chain. It keeps a boat still.

ankle Part of your body which joins your foot and leg.

anorak A jacket with a hood to keep you warm and dry.

ant A very small insect. Hundreds of ants live together.

antelope An animal which looks like a deer.

ape A large animal like a monkey without a tail.

apple A round fruit which people like to eat.

apron A piece of cloth which you wear over your clothes to keep them clean.

opqrstuvwxyz

aquarium A glass tank to keep fish in. You can watch the fish swimming around.

arm The part of your body between your hand and shoulder.

armchair A chair with sides. You rest your arms on the sides.

army Lots of soldiers.

arrow A stick with a point at one end and feathers at the other.

artist A person who paints and draws pictures.

astronaut A person who flies in a spacecraft.

astronomer A person who studies the stars.

axe A sharp tool with a handle. You chop wood with an axe.

abcdefghijklmn

B b

baker A person who bakes and sells bread and cakes.

baby A very young child. A baby cannot walk.

ball An object which is round. You often use a ball to play a game.

badge Something you wear to show that you belong to a certain school or club.

ballet dancer A ballet dancer dances in the ballet. A ballet is dancing which tells a story.

badger A black and white animal which lives in a hole in the ground. A badger is very shy.

balloon A bag filled with air. Some balloons are small, others are large.

bag Something used to hold things. A bag can be made of plastic, paper or material.

banana A long yellow fruit with a thick skin.

opqrstuvwxyz

band A group of people who play musical instruments together.

barn A large building on a farm. Farmers keep things like hay and animals in a barn.

bandage A thin piece of material used for covering a wound. A bandage is usually white.

basin A round bowl for holding liquids.

basket Something to hold things. A basket is made from strips of plaited wood.

barbecue A party outside where food is cooked on a fire.

bat A piece of wood used to hit a ball.

bat A small animal that flies at night. A bat looks like a mouse with wings.

barber A person who cuts hair.

abcdefghijklmn

bath A big container which you can fill with water and sit in. You can wash yourself all over in a bath.

bear A large animal with thick fur. A bear can be black, brown or white.

beard The hair which grows on a man's chin.

bed Something you sleep on. Beds are usually soft and comfortable.

bee A brown and yellow striped insect. A bee collects honey.

beetle An insect with four wings. The front wings are hard and shiny.

bell A bell is hollow. Inside is a ball which hits the side and rings when shaken.

belt A long thin piece of material. You wear it round your waist.

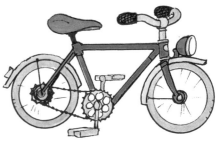

bicycle A machine with two wheels that you ride.

binoculars These are like two telescopes joined together. You look through them to see things which are far away.

opqrstuvwxyz

biscuit   A small crunchy cake.

boat   A small ship. A boat floats on water.

black   The darkest colour of all.

bone   One of the hard white parts of the body of a person or an animal.

blackberry   A small juicy fruit. Blackberries can grow wild.

bonfire   A fire in the garden.

blackbird   A black bird with a yellow beak.

blackbird

book   Pages joined for you to read.

blackboard   A black surface. You
blackboard   can write on it with chalk.

blue   A colour. The sky is blue when the sun shines.

boot   A shoe which covers your ankle.

abcdefghijklmn

bow A curved stick with string. It shoots arrows.

bow A kind of knot. You tie your shoelaces with a bow.

box A container with straight sides. A box is made of cardboard, metal or wood.

boxer A person who fights with his fists.

boy A male child. A boy becomes a man.

branch The part of a tree which grows out from the trunk.

bread A food made from flour.

brick A piece of clay which is made into a block and baked. Bricks are used for building.

bride A woman on her wedding day.

bridegroom A man on his wedding day.

bridge A bridge crosses a road, river or railway. It takes you over to the other side.

broom A brush with a long handle. You sweep away the dust on the floor with a broom.

opqrstuvwxyz

bucket  A container for holding water. A bucket always has a handle.

bud A leaf or a flower before it opens.

budgerigar A small brightly coloured pet bird.

bull The male of any kind of large animal, usually cattle.

bulldozer A big machine which moves lots of earth and rubbish.

bungalow A house with no upstairs. All the rooms of a bungalow are on the ground.

bus A very large car which carries people.

butcher He sells meat.

butter Soft yellow food made from cream.

buttercup A bright yellow wild flower.

butterfly An insect with large coloured wings. A butterfly grows from a caterpillar.

button A small round object. A button fastens your clothes together.

abcdefghijklmn

C c

camel A large animal which lives in the hot dry desert. It carries water in one or two humps on its back.

cabbage A green vegetable which we eat.

canary A small yellow bird which sings. People often keep a canary as a pet.

candle A round piece of wax with string through the middle. The string burns and makes a light.

cage A box or a room made from bars. Animals and birds can be kept in a cage.

canoe A small boat which you paddle.

cake A sweet food which is made from flour, butter, sugar and eggs. A cake is baked in an oven.

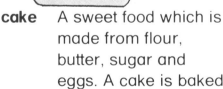

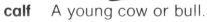

car A motor with four wheels.

calf A young cow or bull.

opqrstuvwxyz

caravan A house on wheels.

carrot A long orange vegetable. A carrot grows in the ground.

castle A big stone building. Castles were built long ago.

Colerp/Mhr **cat** A small furry pet.

caterpillar A small creature which changes into a butterfly.

cave A big hole in a cliff or in a hill.

cello A musical instrument like a big violin.

centipede An insect with lots of legs.

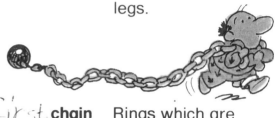

first **chain** Rings which are joined together.

chair A seat for one person to sit on. A chair has *chair* four legs and a back to lean against.

cheese A food which is made from milk.

cherry A small round fruit. A 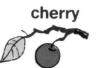 cherry has a stone in the middle.

abcdefghijklmn

chips   Small pieces of potato which are fried.

chess   A game for two people played with chessmen.

chocolate   A brown sweet made from cocoa.

chicken   A young hen. We eat the eggs which a chicken lays.

choir   A group of people who sing together.

chimney   A pipe to let the smoke out of a house. It is on the roof.

church   A building where people go to sing hymns and pray.

chimpanzee   A clever ape.

clarinet   A musical instrument which you blow.

opqrstuvwxyz

claw A sharp hard nail on the foot of an animal or bird.

coat Something you wear over other clothes.

cobweb A thin silky net made by a spider. The spider catches insects in a cobweb.

cliff A high steep rock usually near the sea.

coconut A very large nut which grows on some palm trees.

clock A machine with hands and a face to tell you the time.

comb A comb has teeth for tidying your hair.

comic A paper book with lots of small pictures.

clown A funny man at the circus. A clown has a painted face.

cook A person who cooks food.

abcdefghijklmn

cork A thing to put in the top of bottles to stop the liquid running out.

corn The seeds of plants like wheat, barley and oats. Corn is made into food.

cowboy A man who looks after cattle on a ranch.

cot A small bed with sides. A baby sleeps in a cot.

cowslip A small wild yellow flower.

crab An animal which lives in the sea. It has a hard shell and ten legs.

cottage A small house in the country.

cow The animal which gives us milk.

cracker You pull this and it goes bang. A small present is inside.

opqrstuvwxyz

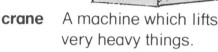

crane A machine which lifts very heavy things.

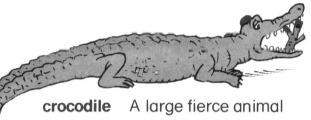

crocodile A large fierce animal which lives in the water and on the land.

crocus A flower which comes out in the spring.

croquet A game played by knocking balls through hoops.

crow A large black bird.

crown Something worn on the head by kings and queens. A crown is often made of gold.

cube A shape which has six sides all the same size.

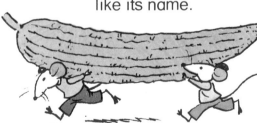

cuckoo A bird which makes a noise which sounds like its name.

cucumber A long green vegetable.

cup A container with a handle. We drink liquid from a cup.

abcdefghijklmn

D d

dentist A person who looks after your teeth.

dagger A kind of knife used for fighting.

daisy A small white wild flower. It is yellow in the middle.

desk A kind of table. You sit at a desk to read and write.

dart A sharp pointed piece of metal with feathers at one end.

dial The face of a watch or clock.

deer A wild animal. A deer has horns and is very shy.

dice Small cubes with numbers on each side. You use dice in many games.

dictionary This book is a dictionary. It tells you what words mean.

opqrstuvwxyz

dinosaur A very large animal which lived thousands of years ago.

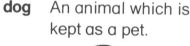

dog An animal which is kept as a pet.

dishwasher A machine which does the washing up.

doll A toy which looks like a baby or a child.

diver A person who swims under the water. Divers wear special suits.

dolphin An animal which lives in the sea. Dolphins are very clever.

doctor A person who helps to make you better when you are ill.

donkey An animal which looks like a small horse. A donkey has long ears.

abcdefghijklmn

door A door opens and shuts and allows you to go into a room or building.

dove A bird which is like a pigeon.

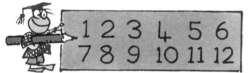

dozen This is another way of saying twelve.

dragon A make-believe animal. Many stories have been written about dragons.

dragonfly A large insect, usually a bright colour.

dress Something worn by women.

drill You use a drill to make holes.

drum A musical instrument which you beat with a stick.

duck A bird which can swim.

opqrstuvwxyz

E e

earthworm A large worm which lives in the earth.

eagle A large bird which eats small animals.

easel A frame made of wood to stand a picture or a blackboard on.

ear You have two ears, one on each side of your head. We hear with our ears.

easter egg An egg made from chocolate.

egg Some animals lay eggs. Babies of these animals are hatched from eggs.

earth The top of the ground. We put plants in the earth.

eight The number between seven and nine.

abcdefghijklmn

elbow The part where your arm bends in the middle.

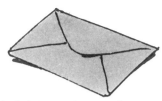

envelope A folded piece of paper. You put a letter in an envelope.

elephant The largest land animal in the world. An elephant has a long nose called a trunk.

excavator A big machine which digs.

eleven The number between ten and twelve.

eye The part of your body you see with.

eyelid The piece of skin which covers your eye.

emu A large bird which cannot fly. Emus live in Australia.

eyelash The hairs along the edge of your eyelids. Eyelashes help to keep dust out of your eyes.

opqrstuvwxyz

F f

fence A kind of wall usually made of wood.

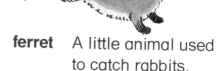

fern A green plant which has feather-like leaves.

face The front part of your head.

fan A machine which blows hot and cold air.

ferret A little animal used to catch rabbits.

ferry A boat which carries people and cars across water.

farmer A person who looks after a farm.

field A piece of land with things growing in it.

feather A lot of fine threads. Birds have feathers.

fingers The five things on the end of your hand.

abcdefghijklmn

fire Something which burns and gives out warmth.

flag A coloured piece of cloth fixed to a stick.

fire engine A large motor car which carries water to put out fires.

flamingo A bird with a long neck and long legs. You often see a flamingo standing in water at the zoo.

fireman A man who rides in a fire engine and puts out fires.

flower The part of a plant which holds the seeds. A flower is usually a bright colour.

fish A creature which lives in water. We eat some fish.

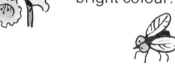

fly A small insect with two wings.

fisherman A person who catches fish.

5

foal A young pony.

five The number between four and six.

foot The part of your body you stand on.

opqrstuvwxyz

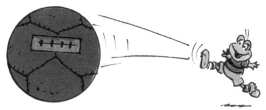

football A leather or plastic ball used in the game of football.

footprint The mark made by your foot when you walk on something soft like sand.

forehead The part of your face between your eyes and your hair.

fork An instrument for picking up food.

fort A strong building. Soldiers used to live in a fort.

fossil The shape of a plant or animal which lived a long time ago. These shapes can still be seen in rocks.

fountain Water which shoots into the air.

four The number between three and five.

fox A small wild animal with a big bushy tail.

frog A creature which can swim in water and jump on land.

abcdefghijklmn

G g

gate A gate is like a door but you see it outside. A gate can be made of wood or iron.

ghost A ghost is supposed to be a dead spirit. No one knows if ghosts are real.

garage A place to keep cars.

garage A place where you get petrol.

garden The land round a house. You grow flowers and vegetables in a garden.

giraffe An animal with a very long neck.

girl A female child.

glass Glass is hard and breaks easily. You can see through glass.

opqrstuvwxyz

glasses 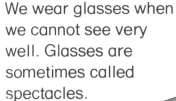 We wear glasses when we cannot see very well. Glasses are sometimes called spectacles.

gnome A little make-believe man who lives underground.

glider An aeroplane without an engine.

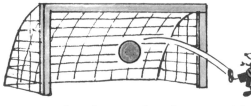

goal A wooden frame with a net. You kick a football into a goal.

globe A round shape like a ball which shows you all the countries of the world.

goat An animal with horns. A goat gives milk.

glove A covering for the hand. Gloves keep our hands warm.

goldfish Fish which are gold in colour.

glue Something which is used to stick things together.

goose A bird which looks like a big white duck.

abcdefghijklmn

gooseberry   A small green berry which you can eat.

grass-hopper   A small insect which jumps.

gorilla   A very large ape.

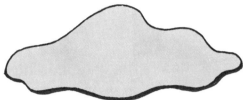

green   The colour of grass.

guinea pig   A small animal kept as a pet.

grape   A sweet juicy fruit. You make wine from grapes.

guitar   A musical instrument with strings.

grapefruit   A bitter fruit like a large yellow orange.

gull   A sea bird.

grass   A green plant.

gun   A weapon used for for shooting.

opqrstuvwxyz

H h

hair Thin threads which grow on your head. Some animals have hair all over their bodies.

hammer A tool for hitting nails.

hamster A small animal like a big mouse. We keep hamsters as pets.

hand Part of your body at the end of your arm.

handcuffs Two metal rings which lock your hands together. Policemen use handcuffs on prisoners.

handker-chief A small piece of cloth you use to blow your nose.

handle Part of anything you hold in your hand. A knife has a handle and so has a door.

handlebars The part of a bicycle you hold onto when riding.

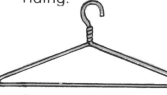

hanger A bent piece of wire with a hook. You hang up your clothes on a hanger.

hare A wild animal like a rabbit.

harp A musical instrument with strings. A harp has the shape of a triangle.

abcdefghijklmn

hat Something you wear on your head.

head All the part of your body above your neck.

headlight The lights on the front of a car or motor cycle.

heart Your heart is inside your body. It pumps blood. You can hear your heart beating.

hedge A kind of fence made from small bushes.

hedgehog A small animal which is very prickly.

heel The back part of your foot.

helicopter An aircraft which can fly straight up and come straight down.

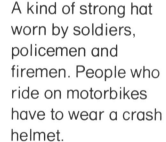

helmet A kind of strong hat worn by soldiers, policemen and firemen. People who ride on motorbikes have to wear a crash helmet.

hen A female bird.

opqrstuvwxyz

heron A bird with long legs which likes standing in water.

herring A small fish found in the sea.

hill A small mountain.

hippo-potamus A very large animal which lives near a river.

hive A small house made of wood. Bees live in a hive.

hoe A garden tool for digging out weeds.

holly A tree with prickly leaves. Some holly trees have red berries.

hook A curved piece of metal. You hang things on a hook.

hoop A circle of wood or plastic. You jump through a hoop or roll it along the ground.

abcdefghijklmn

horn Pointed bones which grow on the heads of some animals.

horn A musical instrument like a big trumpet. You blow a horn to make a sound.

horse A friendly animal. You can ride on a horse.

horseshoe A piece of metal which is fixed to the bottom of a horse's hoof.

hose A long narrow pipe made of rubber or plastic. Water goes through a hose.

hospital A place you go to when you are ill.

house A building where people live.

hut A small building made from wood.

hyena A fierce animal which looks a bit like a wolf.

opqrstuvwxyz

iceberg A very large lump of ice floating in the sea.

ice cream A soft frozen food. Ice cream is made from milk and sugar.

ice skate A special kind of shoe with a sharp metal piece fixed to the bottom.

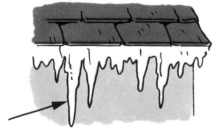

icicle A thin long piece of ice which hangs from a roof in very cold weather.

igloo Eskimos used to live in igloos. An igloo is made from large pieces of hard snow.

insect A small creature with six legs. Ants and flies are insects.

iron Something which is made of metal with a flat part underneath. You make an iron hot and rub it over clothes to smooth them.

island A piece of land which has sea all round it.

ivy A green plant with shiny leaves. Ivy climbs up walls.

abcdefghijklmn

J j

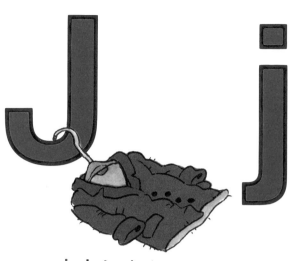

jacket   A short coat.

jack-in-the-box   A toy which looks like a box. When you open the lid a doll pops out.

jack knife   A large pocket knife which has many different blades.

jaguar   A fierce wild animal which looks something like a leopard.

jam   A very sweet food which is made by boiling soft fruit and sugar together.

jay   A bird with blue, brown and pink feathers.

jeans   Trousers made from blue cotton material.

jeep   A very strong kind of motor car. A jeep will go over very rough roads.

opqrstuvwxyz

jelly A wobbly kind of food made from fruit juice and sugar.

jigsaw puzzle A picture which has been cut up into small pieces. These pieces are then fixed together.

jellyfish A sea animal with a soft body. It looks like an umbrella.

jockey A person who rides on a race horse.

jug A container for liquids. A jug has a handle and a special place for the liquid to come out of the top.

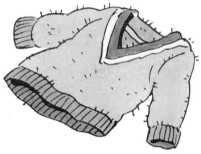

jersey Something you wear on the top part of your body. A jersey is often made from wool.

jewel A special stone which is worth a lot of money. A diamond is a jewel.

jungle A very thick forest found in hot countries.

abcdefghijklmn

K k

key Something you use to open a lock. A key is made of metal.

keyhole A hole in which you put a key to unlock a door.

kid A baby goat.

kangaroo An animal which lives in Australia. A kangaroo hops on its back legs.

kilt A skirt with lots of pleats. People who live in Scotland sometimes wear kilts.

kennel A house for a dog.

kettle A metal container used for boiling water. A kettle always has a handle.

king A man who rules a country. A king is a very important man.

opqrstuvwxyz

kingfisher A bird with bright blue feathers. A kingfisher lives near a river.

kipper A herring which has been dried in smoke.

kitchen The place in a house where you do the cooking.

kite A kind of toy which goes up into the air on a long piece of string.

kitten A baby cat.

knee The middle part of your leg which bends.

knife A sharp piece of metal joined to a handle. You cut things with a knife.

knight A soldier who lived a long time ago.

knot It is made by tying two pieces of string together.

knuckle The part of your finger which bends.

abcdefghijklmn

lace A special kind of string you use to fasten shoes.

ladder A set of steps made from two long planks of wood with small pieces between them. A ladder can be made of metal. You climb up a ladder.

ladle A big spoon which looks like a cup on the end of a long handle.

lamb A baby sheep.

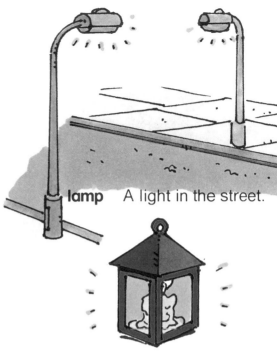

lamp A light in the street.

lantern A lantern is made from metal with glass sides. You usually put a candle in a lantern to give you light.

lark A small bird which sings as it flies in the sky.

lasso A rope with a loop on the end. You catch horses and cattle with a lasso.

opqrstuvwxyz

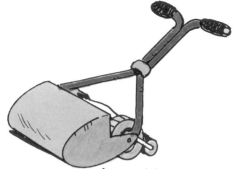

lawnmower A machine used for cutting grass.

leaf It is green and grows on plants and trees.

leap frog A game in which one person jumps over another.

leg We have two legs. We walk with them. They are joined to our body.

lemon A yellow, very sour, fruit.

leopard A fierce animal which looks like a large cat.

letter A message which is written down on paper and then put in an envelope.

letter A mark that stands for a sound we say. Words are made from letters.

lettuce A plant with big green leaves. You eat lettuce without cooking it.

abcdefghijklmn

lifeboat A special fast boat which rescues people in the sea.

lighthouse A tall tower with a big flashing light. A lighthouse helps ships to know where they are in the dark.

lion A large wild animal found in Africa and other countries.

litter bin A container in which to put your rubbish.

lizard A small animal with four legs and a long tail.

lobster A small sea animal with a hard shell and five pairs of legs. The front legs have sharp claws.

log A round piece of wood which has been cut from a tree.

lollipop A large sweet on the end of a stick.

luggage All the cases and bags you take with you when you go away.

opqrstuvwxyz

Mm

marbles Small pretty balls made of glass.

magnet A piece of metal which can pull other pieces of metal to it.

marionette A puppet which you move with strings.

magnifying glass A glass which can make things look much bigger than they really are.

mask Something you wear over your face to hide it or protect it.

magpie A black and white bird which is very noisy.

mast A tall pole on the deck of a boat. It holds the sail up.

mallet A wooden hammer.

map A drawing which shows you how to find your way to somewhere.

mat A piece of thick material you put on the floor.

abcdefghijklmn

match A thin piece of wood with a special tip. This tip makes fire when you strike it against something.

mattress A very thick pad which goes on a bed.

maze A place with lots of paths all crossing each other. You can get lost in a maze.

meat Parts of an animal used for food.

medal A piece of metal like a coin. You are given a medal if you do something brave.

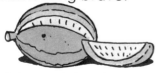

melon A large juicy fruit.

mermaid A make-believe sea fairy with the tail of a fish.

merry-go-round A large wooden platform with wooden animals on it. A merry-go-round is sometimes called a roundabout.

microphone An instrument which makes sound louder.

microscope An instrument which you use to look at very small things.

opqrstuvwxyz

milk   A white liquid food.

mink   A small animal with soft fur. The fur of a mink is very valuable.

minnow   A very small fish.

mirror   A piece of glass with silver painted on the back. You can see yourself in a mirror.

mitten   A covering for the hand. A mitten is like a glove but with one place for all the fingers and one place for the thumb.

mole   A small animal which lives under the ground.

monkey   A small animal which can climb trees and swing from branch to branch. A monkey can be very clever.

moon   It looks like a large bright light in the sky at night. The moon seems to change its shape each night.

mop   A sponge on a long handle. You clean the floor with a mop.

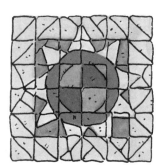

mosaic   Lots of little pieces of glass or stone put together to make a picture.

abcdefghijklmn

mosque A place where Muslims worship.

mosquito A small flying insect.

motor boat A boat that is run by a motor.

motor cycle Something which looks like a large heavy bicycle. It is run by a motor.

mountain A very high rocky hill.

mouse A small animal with a long tail.

mouth The opening in your face where you put your food and drink.

mug A big cup which usually has straight sides.

mushroom A small plant. When it is growing in the ground it looks like an umbrella.

opqrstuvwxyz

N n

net Material which has lots of holes in. You use a net to catch fish.

nail A small thin piece of metal with a flat top and a point at the other end.

net Net can be made with wire. You use this to make a fence or a cage.

neck The part of the body which joins the chest to the head.

nettle A weed which stings you if you touch the leaves.

necklace A piece of jewellery worn round the neck.

newspaper Large printed sheets of paper which tell you what has happened.

nectarine A sweet juicy fruit which looks like a peach.

needle A thin piece of metal with a sharp point at one end and a hole at the other.

newt A small creature with a long tail. It can live on land and in water.

nest A place where birds lay their eggs. Most birds build their own nests.

nib The point of a pen. The ink comes through the nib when you write.

abcdefghijklmn

note book   A book of paper which you write in.

nightgown   Something girls wear when they go to bed.

nine   The number between eight and ten.

nun   A woman who lives in a convent and prays to God a lot of the time.

ninepins   A game where you try to knock over wooden sticks with a ball.

nurse   A person who looks after sick people.

noose   A circle of rope made by tying a slip knot. When you pull the long end of the rope the loop gets smaller.

nut   The seed of a tree.

nut   A piece of metal which you screw on to the end of a bolt.

nutcrackers   Something you use to break the hard shell of a nut so that you can eat the inside.

nose   Part of your face you breathe through. You have two holes in your nose. These are called nostrils.

nuthatch   A small pretty bird which likes to eat nuts.

opqrstuvwxyz

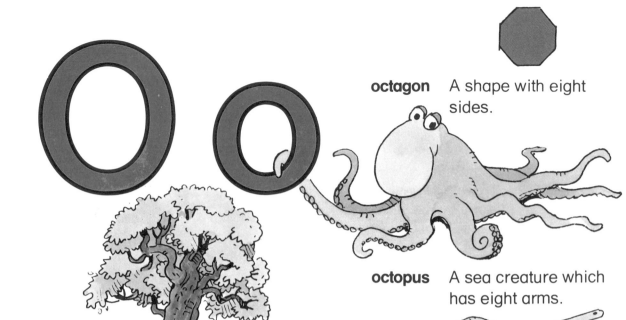

octagon A shape with eight sides.

octopus A sea creature which has eight arms.

oak A large tree which lives for a very long time.

oar A pole with a flat end. You use two oars to row a boat.

oboe A musical instrument.

observatory A building with special telescopes inside for watching stars.

omelette A food which is made by beating eggs and frying them.

one the lowest number.

onion A round vegetable which grows under the ground. An onion has a very strong smell.

orange Orange is a colour. It is also a fruit.

orchard A place where lots of fruit trees grow.

O o

abcdefghijklmn

orchestra Lots of people playing musical instruments.

orchid Brightly coloured flowers. Large ones grow in hot countries or in a hot greenhouse in colder countries. Small orchids grow wild.

organ A big musical instrument with black and white notes like a piano.

osprey A sea eagle.

ostrich A very large bird which cannot fly. An ostrich has long legs and can run very fast.

otter A fish-eating animal which lives near a river. It is not easy to see an otter.

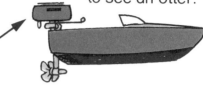

outboard motor A motor which goes on the outside of a boat.

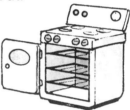

oven The part of a cooker where you put food in to bake.

overalls Something you wear on top of your clothes to keep them clean.

owl A bird which usually flies at night. Owls catch and eat small animals.

opqrstuvwxyz

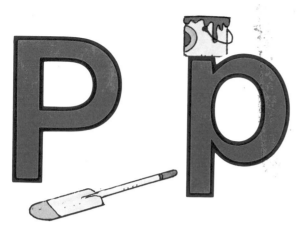

paddle A long thin piece of wood with a flat piece each end. You use a paddle to make a canoe go along in the water.

paddock A small field.

padlock A lock which is movable.

page One side of a piece of paper in a book.

pagoda A Chinese temple.

pail Another name for a bucket.

paint A liquid you paint on something to make it a different colour.

palm A tree which grows in hot countries.

palm The inside surface of your hand.

pancake A food you make with eggs, flour and milk. A pancake is very thin.

panda A small animal with reddish-brown fur. A giant panda is a large black and white animal which lives in China.

P p

abcdefghijklmn

pane A thin piece of glass which goes in a window frame.

panther An animal like a leopard.

paper clip A piece of bent metal which fixes sheets of paper together.

parachute A large round piece of cloth with strings attached to the edge. You use a parachute when you have to fall a long way in the sky.

parasole An umbrella which shades you from the sun.

parcel Something wrapped up in paper and tied with string or sticky tape.

park A large garden usually in a town. People and children can walk and play in a park.

parrot A bird with bright feathers. People sometimes keep parrots as pets because you can teach them to talk.

passenger A person who rides in a car, bus, train or aeroplane.

patchwork Lots of little pieces of material sewn together to make a pretty cover.

path A road which you walk on. Cars and bicycles do not ride on a path.

opqrstuvwxyz

paw The soft foot of an animal.

pea A vegetable which looks like a little green ball. Lots of peas grow together in a green case called a pod.

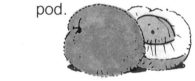

peach A sweet juicy fruit with a big seed in the middle.

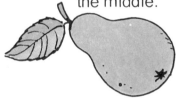

pear The juicy fruit of the pear tree.

pebble Small round stones. You can find lots of pebbles on a beach.

peg A piece of wood or plastic with a metal spring. You hang the washing up with pegs.

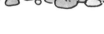

Pekingese A small dog with very short legs.

pelican A large water bird. A pelican has a big pouch underneath its beak.

pen Something which writes in ink.

pencil A thin piece of wood with lead down the middle. You write and draw with a pencil. You can rub it out if you wish.

pendulum A heavy weight found in some big clocks. A pendulum swings backwards and forwards and makes the clock keep time.

abcdefghijklmn

penguin A bird which lives in the Antarctic. A penguin can swim but it cannot fly.

pennant A long thin flag which is pointed at one end.

perch A wooden bar in a cage for a bird to sit on.

perfume A sweet smelling liquid made from the petals of flowers.

periscope An instrument used in submarines. A periscope lets you see what is happening on the top of the water.

petal Part of a flower.

petrol The liquid used in cars to make the engine go.

petticoat Something which can be worn under a dress.

pheasant A bird which lives in woods. Some people shoot pheasants and eat them.

photograph A picture made by a camera.

photo-grapher A person who takes pictures with a camera.

opqrstuvwxyz

pianist A person who plays a piano.

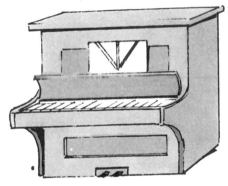

piano A musical instrument. You hit the black and white keys to make the sound.

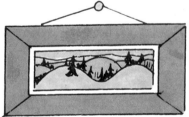

piccolo A musical instrument like a small flute. A piccolo makes a very high sound.

picture A drawing, painting or photograph. Sometimes you hang a picture on the wall.

pie Something you eat made with pastry on the outside and fruit or meat in the middle.

pig An animal which is kept on a farm. When we eat pig we call it pork.

pigeon A bird which can be wild or tame. Pigeons are clever and can find their way home from a long way away.

pike A rather fierce fish found in rivers.

pill A small ball which is medicine. A pill is small enough to swallow.

pillar A wooden or stone post which helps to hold up a building.

abcdefghijklmn

pillar box A bright red box in the street to post your letters in.

pillow A bag filled with soft material. You put your head on a pillow when you sleep.

pilot A person who flies an aeroplane.

pin A small thin piece of metal like a nail.

pineapple A large fruit which grows in hot countries. It has a very thick skin.

pink A colour made from red and white.

pipe A hollow tube that liquids run through.

pipe You can put tobacco in a pipe and smoke it.

pirate A person who used to rob treasure from a ship at sea. You read about pirates in story books.

pistol A small gun.

pitchfork A fork with a long handle and only two spikes. You lift hay with a pitchfork.

pizza A flat cake of dough with a tasty topping. It comes from Italy.

opqrstuvwxyz

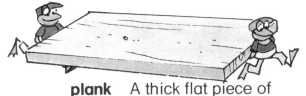

plank A thick flat piece of wood.

plaster A piece of material with sticky ends. You put plaster on a cut to stop it from getting dirty.

plate A flat dish. You put your food on a plate.

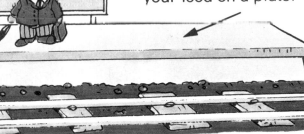

platform Part of the floor which is higher than the rest. You can also see a platform at a railway station. It is always higher than the railway lines.

plug A piece of rubber or plastic you put in the hole in the sink to stop the water from running away.

plug All electric machines have a plug on the end of the flex. This joins it to the electricity supply.

plum A soft juicy fruit with a stone in the middle.

plumber A person who fixes water pipes.

pocket A small bag fixed to your coat, trousers or dress. You can keep your money in a pocket.

polar bear A large white bear.

pole A long round stick.

abcdefghijklmn

polecat   A small animal like a weasel.

police   People who see that other people do not break the law.

polo   A game played by people sitting on horses and hitting a ball with a stick.

pony   A small horse.

poodle   A small dog with curly hair.

poppy   A bright red flower which grows wild.

porcupine   An animal like a giant rat covered with long prickles.

porpoise   A sea animal like a small whale.

porthole   A window in a ship. Portholes are usually round.

postcard   A small piece of card. You write a message on a postcard and send it in the post.

postman   A person who delivers our letters.

opqrstuvwxyz

post office A place to buy stamps and to post parcels.

pot A container used to hold liquid. You make tea in a tea pot.

potato A vegetable which grows in the ground. Most people like potatoes to eat.

prince The son of a king or queen.

princess The daughter of a king or queen.

prison A building where people who do wrong things are locked up.

projector A machine which is used to show films.

propeller A blade which goes round and round very fast to make an aeroplane or ship go forward.

puddle A small pool of water.

puffin A bird which has a beak like a parrot. Puffins live near the sea.

abcdefghijklmn

pump A machine which pushes air or liquid into a container. You use a pump to put air into your bicycle tyre.

pyjamas A jacket and trousers people wear in bed.

pupil The black part of your eye.

pylon A big metal tower which holds up electric cables.

puppet A doll moved by string or by your hand.

puppy A young dog.

pyramid A solid building which looks like four triangles meeting at a point on the top.

purple A colour made with red and blue.

purse A small bag to put your money in.

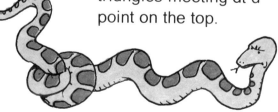

python A very big snake.

opqrstuvwxyz

Q q

quads Four children born to the same mother at the same time.

queen A woman who rules a country.

quarry A place where stone is dug out of the earth.

quill A pen made from a feather.

quay A place where ships are tied to the land.

quilt A warm cover to go on top of a bed.

abcdefghijklmn

R r

racket A bat with strings. You play tennis with a racket.

radiator A radiator is made of metal. It usually has hot water inside. This keeps a room warm.

rabbit A small animal with long ears. Some rabbits are tame and live in hutches but most of them are wild.

radishes Small red vegetables which you eat raw in a salad.

raccoon A small wild animal. A raccoon has a long bushy tail with black rings.

raft Bits of wood fixed together to make a flat kind of boat.

race track A path where a race is run.

rain Drops of water which fall out of the clouds.

opqrstuvwxyz

rainbow A band of beautiful colours sometimes seen in the sky.

rattle snake A poisonous snake. When it shakes its tail it rattles.

rake A garden tool with a long handle and metal teeth.

raven A big black bird with very shiny feathers.

ram A male sheep.

razor Something very sharp used to shave hair off your skin.

raspberry A small soft red fruit.

recorder A musical instrument which you blow.

rat An animal which looks like a large mouse.

rectangle A shape with four sides.

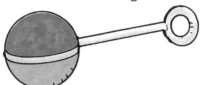

rattle A toy for a baby.

red A colour. Your lips are red.

abcdefghijklmn

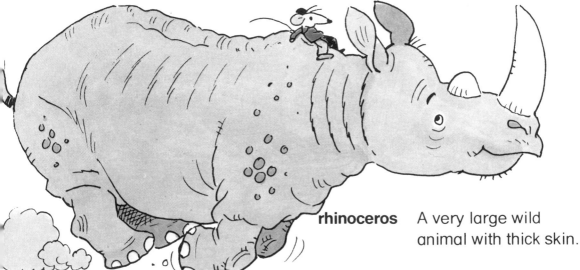

rhinoceros A very large wild animal with thick skin.

rhubarb A plant with thick red stalks. We cook the stalks and eat them. We do not eat the leaves.

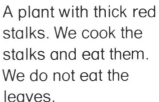

refrigerator A cupboard which is made cold by electricity or gas. The cold helps to keep food fresh.

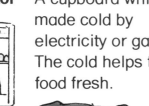

ribbon A narrow piece of silk or velvet. Girls sometimes wear ribbon in their hair.

reindeer A kind of deer with very large horns. Reindeer live in cold countries.

ribs The bones in your chest.

rice The hard seeds of a plant which grows in hot countries. When you cook rice it goes soft.

reins Leather straps used to guide a horse.

revolver A kind of pistol.

ring A piece of metal in the shape of a circle. You wear a ring on your finger.

opqrstuvwxyz

river   Water which flows down from the hills into the sea.

road   A hard path made for cars and lorries.

robin   A small bird with a red breast.

rock   A very large stone.

rock   A thin stick of sweet.

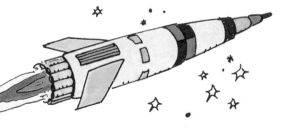

rocket   A machine which is shot up into space.

rocking chair   A chair which goes backwards and forwards when you sit in it.

rocking horse   A toy horse which goes backwards and forwards when you sit on it.

rod   A thin piece of wood. It usually has very thin string on one end for fishing.

roller skates   Special boots which have wheels on them.

roof   The covering on top of a building. The roof of a house is often made of tiles.

abcdefghijklmn

root The part of any plant which grows under the ground.

rope Very thick string.

rose A flower which has a lovely smell.

roundabout Something you see at the fair. You sit on it and go round and round.

rowing boat A boat which needs oars to move it along.

rubber Soft material you use to rub out drawings or writing which are wrong.

rubber band A piece of very thin rubber joined together to make a circle. A rubber band stretches.

ruby A red jewel.

rudder A piece of wood or metal on the back of a boat. A rudder moves to make the boat go different ways.

rug A small piece of carpet, sometimes called a mat.

rung A step on a ladder.

opqrstuvwxyz

S s

sand   Tiny grains of rock. You see lots of sand at the seaside and in deserts.

sandwich   Two pieces of bread and butter with some tasty food in between.

sack   A large bag made of cloth.

sausage   Meat minced up and put into thin skins.

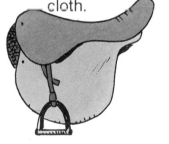

saw   A metal blade with sharp teeth down one side and a handle on the end. You cut wood with a saw.

saddle   A leather seat which goes on the back of a horse. A rider sits in the saddle.

saxophone   A musical instrument you blow.

sail   A piece of strong material fixed to the mast of a boat. The sail catches the wind and makes the boat move.

scarecrow   Something which is put into a field to frighten the birds. It usually looks like a person but it is not.

salmon   A big fish which has pink flesh.

abcdefghijklmn

scarf A long thin piece of material you wear round your neck to keep you warm.

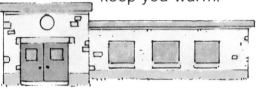

school A place where you go to learn.

schooner A large sailing ship.

scissors These are like two knives fixed together. You cut material and paper with scissors.

scorpion A creature like a big spider. A scorpion has a long tail and it can sting you.

screw A thin piece of metal like a nail but it has grooves in it.

screwdriver You use this to put screws into wood.

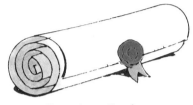

scroll A roll of paper.

scrubbing brush A brush without a handle.

scythe A tool which has a long blade. You cut long grass with a scythe.

seagull A bird you see by the sea.

opqrstuvwxyz

seahorse A little sea animal which has no legs and a curly tail.

seal A large sea animal. A seal can live on land.

searchlight A very big torch which can shine high in the sky.

seashell The hard covering of oysters and other sea animals. Sea shells can be found by the sea. It is what is left after the animal has died.

seat Something you sit on.

seat belt A strong piece of material which is fixed to the side of a car. You fix it round you to keep you safe.

seaweed A plant which grows in the sea. Seaweed is very slippery.

seed The part of a plant from which new plants grow.

seesaw A long piece of wood put over a block of wood. You can go up and down on a seesaw.

abcdefghijklmn

semicircle Half a circle.

sentry A soldier standing on guard.

seven The number between six and eight.

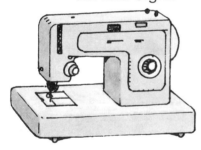

sewing machine A machine which sews things together. It is much quicker than sewing by hand.

shadow A dark patch on the ground made when a person or object gets in the way of the light.

shampoo A liquid soap you use to wash your hair.

shark A large sea fish with sharp teeth. Some sharks can eat people.

shawl A piece of material worn round your shoulders to keep you warm.

shears Very large scissors for cutting grass.

shed A wooden hut.

sheep An animal which gives us wool.

opqrstuvwxyz

sheet A large piece of material used on a bed.

sheik An arab chief.

shelf A piece of wood fixed to a wall. You put books and ornaments on a shelf.

shellfish A sea animal which has a shell. An oyster is a shellfish.

shepherd A person who looks after sheep.

shield A flat piece of metal wood or plastic which you hold in front of yourself to stop things hurting you.

ship A large boat.

shirt A piece of clothing you wear on the top part of your body.

shoe Something you wear on your feet.

shop A place you go to when you want to buy something.

abcdefghijklmn

shorts Trousers which come above your knee.

shoulder The part of your body where your arm joins your body.

shovel A tool which is like a spade only bigger.

shower A little bit of rain.

shower A spray of water from above. You can wash yourself in a shower.

shrew A little animal with fur like velvet. A shrew is very shy.

shrimp A small sea animal.

sieve A container which has has a bottom with lots of holes in it. If you put earth in a sieve and shake it all the earth falls through the holes and the stones stay in the sieve.

signpost Writing on a piece of wood or metal which tells you where to go.

silkworm A caterpillar that makes a thin silk thread.

silo A tall tower used to keep animal food in.

opqrstuvwxyz

sink   A place in the kitchen where you wash the dirty dishes.

six   The number which comes before seven and after five.

skeleton   All the bones in your body.

skis   Two long pieces of wood. You fasten your boots to skis when you want to slide down the snow.

skipping rope   A rope with a handle at each end. You turn the rope to skip.

skirt   A piece of clothing worn by girls and women.

skull   The bone in your head.

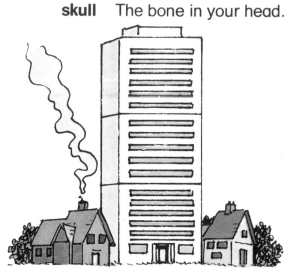

skyscraper   A very tall building.

sledge   Something you sit on and slide down a hill when it is covered with snow.

sledge-hammer   A very heavy hammer which will break a rock.

abcdefghijklmn

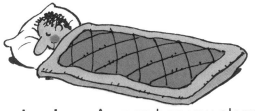

sleeping bag A warm bag you sleep in when you go camping.

smoke A kind of dirty cloud which comes from a fire.

slide A long piece of smooth metal you can slide down. First you have to climb a ladder.

snail A small garden creature which has a shell on its back.

snake A long thin creature with no legs. Not all snakes are dangerous.

sling A piece of material you tie round your arm and neck if you have broken your arm.

snorkel A tube which you use if you want to swim underwater. One end goes in your mouth and the other stays above the water.

slipper A soft shoe worn in the house.

slug A large snail without a shell.

snout The nose of a pig.

opqrstuvwxyz

snow   Frozen rain.

snowman   A man made out of snow.

snowplough   A machine which can push lots of snow off the road.

soap   Something you use with water when you want to get yourself clean.

sock   Clothing you wear on your feet.

sofa   A long seat which is soft to sit on.

soldier   A man in the army.

sole   The bottom part of your foot or your shoe.

sombrero   A big hat worn by people in Mexico.

spacecraft   A machine which can go up into space.

abcdefghijklmn

spade A tool for digging the garden.

spaghetti Long thin pieces of white food made from flour, eggs and water.

sparrow A little brown and white bird often seen in gardens.

spear A long handle with a sharp piece of metal at one end. A spear is used to hurt people and animals.

speed-ometer An instrument in a car which tells you how fast you are going.

spider An insect with eight legs. It catches flies in a web.

spine The bones in your back. The spine is made of lots of little bones joined together.

spinning wheel A big wheel which is driven by the foot to spin wool.

spire The pointed top of a church steeple.

springboard The piece of wood hanging over the edge of a swimming pool. You jump or dive off the springboard.

opqrstuvwxyz

sprinkler Something used to water gardens.

spur A piece of sharp metal which is worn by cowboys on their boots. Spurs are used to make the horse go faster.

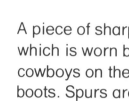

square A shape with four equal straight sides.

stadium Rows and rows of seats built round a big space. People watch sports in a stadium.

stag A male deer.

squirrel A small grey or red animal with a long bushy tail. A squirrel lives in trees.

stage A platform where people act.

stagecoach A large coach which was pulled by several horses. Stagecoaches used to carry passengers.

stable A house for a horse.

abcdefghijklmn

stairs The steps in a building for getting up or down to the next floor.

star A bright light we see in the sky at night.

starfish A flat sea animal with five arms. This makes it look like a star.

station The place where trains stop to pick up people and to let people off the train.

steak A thick slice of lean meat

stem The thin green part of a plant. The flower grows on top of the stem.

stick A long thin piece of wood.

stomach This is like a big bag in your body. The food you eat goes into your stomach.

stone A small piece of rock.

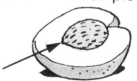

stone The hard seed inside some fruit.

stool A little seat with no back.

opqrstuvwxyz

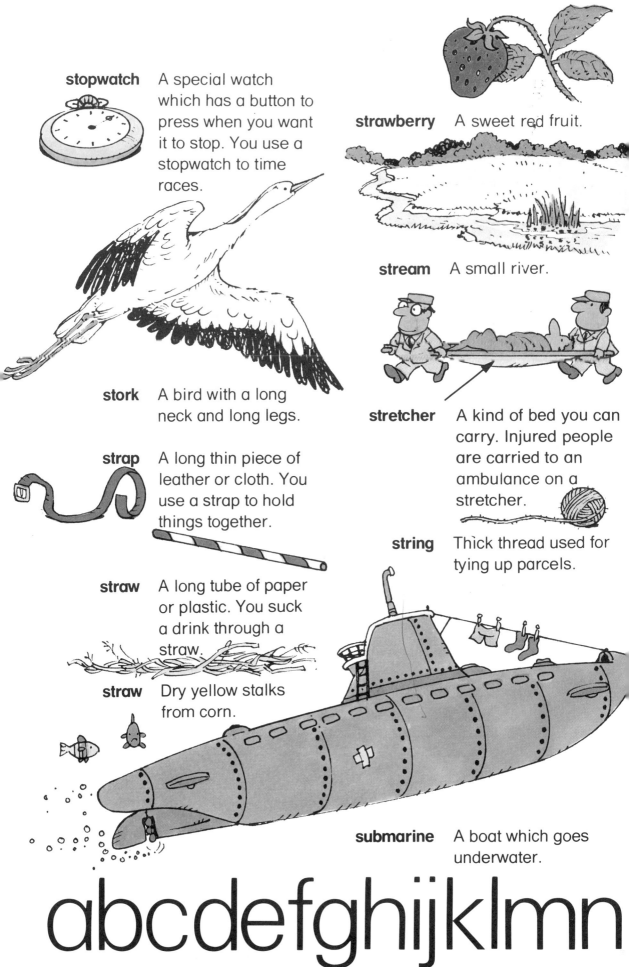

stopwatch A special watch which has a button to press when you want it to stop. You use a stopwatch to time races.

strawberry A sweet red fruit.

stream A small river.

stork A bird with a long neck and long legs.

stretcher A kind of bed you can carry. Injured people are carried to an ambulance on a stretcher.

strap A long thin piece of leather or cloth. You use a strap to hold things together.

string Thick thread used for tying up parcels.

straw A long tube of paper or plastic. You suck a drink through a straw.

straw Dry yellow stalks from corn.

submarine A boat which goes underwater.

abcdefghijklmn

sun The sun shines in the sky and gives us light and heat.

sunflower A bright yellow flower. Sunflowers can grow taller than a man.

sunglasses Dark glasses which shade our eyes from the sun.

surfboard A long flat board you use to ride on the waves.

swan A large water bird with a long neck and webbed feet.

sweet A food made from sugar.

swing A seat hanging from chains or ropes. You sit on the seat and move backwards and forwards.

sword A long sharp blade with a handle at one end. A sword is used for fighting.

swordfish A fish which looks as though it has a sword on the end of its nose.

opqrstuvwxyz

T t

table A piece of furniture with a flat top and four legs.

tadpole A very young frog or toad.

tail The part of an animal's body which sticks out at the back.

tambourine A small kind of drum which rattles when you shake it.

tangerine A small juicy fruit like an orange.

tank A very heavy car made from special metal. There are guns in a tank.

tanker A ship which can carry oil or other liquids.

tap You turn a tap to make water run out.

tape recorder A machine which can record sound on to plastic tape. This machine can also play the sound back.

tart A small piece of pastry with jam or fruit in the middle.

abcdefghijklmn

ten The number between nine and eleven.

10

taxi A car that you have to pay to ride in.

tent A house made out of material and kept up with poles.

teeth The hard bones in your mouth. You can bite food with your teeth.

tentacle A long bendy arm. An octopus has eight tentacles.

telephone An instrument you speak into. It carries your voice through electric wires to someone far away.

telescope Something which makes objects far away look much nearer.

tepee A Red Indian tent which goes up to a point.

television An instrument which is able to bring pictures and sound through the air from a long way away. You can see these pictures when you switch on.

test tube A thin glass container which is open at one end.

opqrstuvwxyz

thermo-meter An instrument used for finding out what your temperature is when you are ill.

thermos A container which keeps things hot.

thimble A small metal or plastic cover which protects the top of your finger when you are sewing.

thistle A plant which is prickly.

thorn A sharp point which grows on some plants and trees.

3

three The number between two and four.

throne A special kind of seat for kings and queens.

thrush A bird which sings. It has a speckled breast.

thumb The short thick finger you have on each hand.

ticket A small piece of paper you get when you pay to ride on a bus or go into the cinema.

tie A strip of material which you wear round your neck under the collar of your shirt.

tom tom   A drum which you beat with your hands.

tongs   A tool used to pick up things.

tiger   A fierce animal like a big striped cat.

toad   An animal like a frog. A toad lives on the land most of the time.

tongue   A thick piece of flesh inside your mouth. Your tongue moves when you talk and eat.

toast   Bread which you have cooked so it is golden brown on both sides.

tooth   One of your teeth.

toes   The parts of your body on the end of your feet.

toothbrush   A small brush for scrubbing your teeth.

toothpaste   A special paste for cleaning your teeth. You put the toothpaste on your toothbrush.

tomato   A red juicy vegetable.

opqrstuvwxyz

torch A light you can carry about and switch on and off.

towel A cloth for drying yourself when you have washed.

toreador A man who fights bulls.

tower A tall building.

tortoise An animal which walks very slowly. It has a thick shell on its back.

tractor A farm vehicle with big back wheels. A tractor can pull heavy things.

toucan A bird with bright feathers and a very big beak.

trailer Something on wheels which can be pulled by a car or lorry.

abcdefghijklmn

train A lot of carriages pulled by an engine.

tramp A person with no home who walks from place to place.

trampoline A piece of strong material stretched over a metal frame. You can jump up and down on a trampoline.

trap Something you catch things in.

trapeze A short bar hung between two ropes. You swing on a trapeze.

tray A flat piece of wood, plastic or metal. You carry plates and cups on a tray.

tree A large plant with a trunk and leaves.

trench A long narrow ditch.

triangle A shape with three sides.

tricycle A cycle with three wheels.

opqrstuvwxyz

triplets Three children born to the same mother at the same time.

tripod Three metal legs joined at one end. You can put a camera on a tripod.

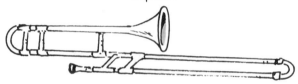

trombone A musical instrument.

trousers A piece of clothing which covers your legs.

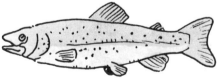

trout A fish which lives in rivers.

trumpet A musical instrument.

trunk The main part of a tree.

T-shirt A shirt with short sleeves and no collar.

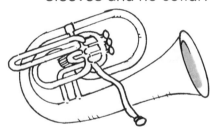

tuba A very big musical instrument.

tugboat A small strong boat which can pull other boats.

abcdefghijklmn

tunnel A passage built under the ground.

turban A long scarf you wind round and round your head.

turkey A large bird we often eat at Christmas.

turnip A white round hard vegetable which grows under the ground.

turtle A turtle has a shell. It lives on land and in water.

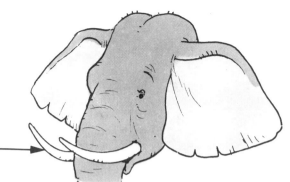

tusks Long pointed teeth that some animals have at the sides of their mouths.

twig A very small branch of a tree.

twins Two children who are born at the same time to the same mother.

two The number between one and three.

typewriter A machine which prints letters when you press the keys.

opqrstuvwxyz

U u V v

umbrella Something you hold over your head to keep off the rain.

underpass A road which goes under a bridge or another road.

unicorn A pretend animal that looks something like a horse with a horn sticking out of the middle of its head.

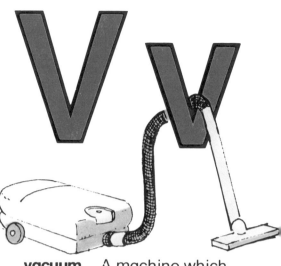

vacuum cleaner A machine which picks up dirt from the floor.

van A car with no windows at the back. A van can be large or small.

vase A container for flowers.

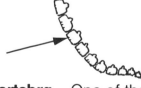

vertebra One of the small bones in your back.

abcdefghijklmn

vest A piece of your clothing you wear next to your skin.

violin A musical instrument with strings.

waistcoat A coat without sleeves.

waiter A man who serves food in a restaurant.

volcano A mountain with a hole in the top. Sometimes hot ash comes out of the hole.

waitress A woman who serves food in a restaurant.

vulture A large bird which eats dead animals.

wall Something built of bricks or stones. Houses have walls.

opqrstuvwxyz

wallet A small case for holding your money.

wallpaper Paper with a pattern on it used to cover walls.

walnut A nut with a hard shell.

walrus An animal which looks like a seal but it is larger. A walrus has two tusks.

wand A thin stick used by a magician.

wardrobe A large cupboard to keep your clothes in.

warehouse A very large building. All kinds of things are kept in a warehouse before they go to the shops.

washing machine A machine for washing clothes.

wasp An insect which can sting you.

waste paper basket A basket kept in a house or office. You throw your rubbish in this basket.

watch Something you wear to tell you the time.

waterfall Lots of water falling from a high place.

abcdefghijklmn

weasel A small animal with a long neck. A weasel eats snakes and rabbits.

weather-cock Two pieces of metal in the shape of a cross. A weathercock blows round in the wind and shows you which way the wind is blowing.

web A spider spins a web.

whale A large animal which lives in the sea.

wheat A kind of grain. Flour is made from wheat.

wheel A circle made of wood or metal. Cars have four wheels. They go round and make the car move.

whip A strap with a handle.

whiskers The hairs which grow on a man's face.

whiskers Hairs which grow out of the side of a cat's or a dog's face.

whistle Something you blow to make a high sound.

wig Hair which you put on over your own hair.

wigwam A kind of tent.

opqrstuvwxyz

willow A tree which has branches which bend over.

witch A woman who is supposed to be magic.

windmill A machine which is worked by the wind.

wizard A man who is supposed to be magic.

window A hole in the wall of a building. Glass covers the hole.

wolf A wild animal which looks like a dog.

wing The part of the body of birds and insects which moves. The wings are used for flying.

woodpecker A bird which uses its beak to make a hole in a tree.

worm A long thin animal with a soft body and no legs.

wishbone A bone in the front of a chicken.

wren A very small bird.

abcdefghijklmn

X x

x-ray A photograph which shows what the inside of your body looks like.

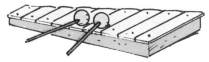

xylophone A row of thin pieces of wood which make a sound when you hit them.

Y y

yacht A boat with sails.

yak An animal like an ox with long hair.

yellow A colour. Daffodils are yellow.

yo-yo A toy which spins up and down on a string.

Z z

zebra A wild animal with black and white stripes. Zebras come from Africa.

zip Something which fastens two bits of material together.

zoo A place where wild animals are kept so that people can look at them.

opqrstuvwxyz

All the words in this part of the dictionary tell you what the animals are doing. All doing words are called verbs. Look carefully at what the animals are doing in these lovely pictures, this will help you to read the word which is written underneath.

All the words are in the same order as the alphabet. This makes it easier for you to look things up. Perhaps you can see if you can do all the things the animals do in these pictures.

Remember these doing words are called verbs.

abcdefghijklmn

opqrstuvwxyz

acting

bouncing

baking

brushing

balancing

building

batting

burning

blowing

abcdefghijklmn

carving

chopping

cleaning

chasing

climbing

opqrstuvwxyz

combing

crashing

cooking

crossing

counting

cutting

abcdefghijklmn

dancing

dressing

dIgging

drinking

diving

drawing

driving

opqrstuvwxyz

eating

filming

emptying

filling

falling

fishing

fighting

floating

flying

abcdefghijklmn

galloping

hitting

hanging

hoeing

helping

hopping

hugging

hiding

opqrstuvwxyz

icing

juggling

ironing

itching

jumping

abcdefghijklmn

kicking

knitting

kissing

knocking

kneeling

opqrstuvwxyz

laughing

listening

lying

licking

loading

abcdefghijklmn

marching

mending

milking

measuring

mixing

melting

moving

opqrstuvwxyz

packing

picking

paddling

playing

painting

peeling

ploughing

abcdefghijklmn

polishing

praying

posting

pumping

pouring

pushing

queuing

opqrstuvwxyz

racing

riding

raining

rocking

rolling

reading

rowing

running

rescuing

abcdefghijklmn

sailing

shaving

sawing

shivering

scrubbing

shooting

sewing

opqrstuvwxyz

shopping

skating

sleeping

singing

sliding

sitting

smelling

abcdefghijklmn

smoking

sweeping

snowing

swimming

spinning

swinging

stroking

opqrstuvwxyz

threading

touching

throwing

typing

abcdefghijklmn

walking

washing

watching

watering

weighing

winding

wrapping

writing

I am
a

yawning

zipping

opqrstuvwxyz

Find ten things hidden in this picture.

abcdefghijklmn

opqrstuvwxyz

How many things can you find in this picture beginning with the letter S. Using this dictionary, see if you can write down their names.

abcdefghijklmn

How many things can you find in this picture beginning with the letter P. Using this dictionary, see if you can write down their names.

NO RIDING IN THE PARK

opqrstuvwxyz

What are these animals doing? Can you find the words in this dictionary? See if you can write them down.

abcdefghijklmn

opqrstuvwxyz

Here are twenty-six pictures. Can you write down their names and put them in alphabetical order? Use the alphabet at the bottom to help you. You should begin like this: apple, bear, cat.

abcdefghijklmn

opqrstuvwxyz

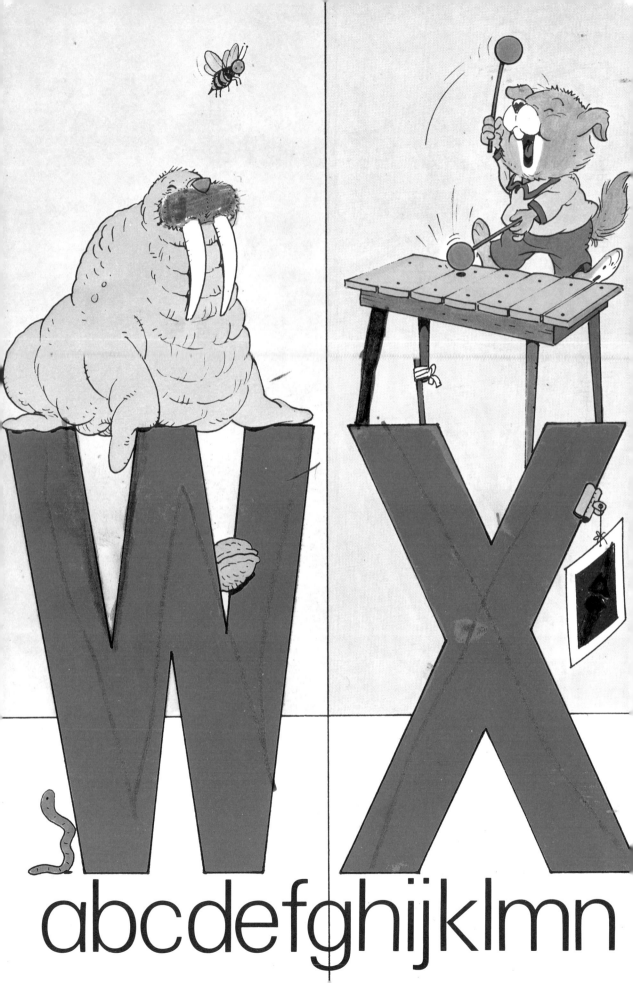

W X

abcdefghijklmn